All Kinds of Animals

Sally Hewitt

CHILDREN'S PRESS®

A Division of Grolier Publishing

NEW YORK • LONDON • HONG KONG • SYDNEY
DANBURY, CONNECTICUT

First published by Franklin Watts 1998

First American edition 1998 by
Children's Press
A Division of Grolier Publishing
90 Sherman Turnpike
Danbury, CT 06816

Visit Children's Press on the Internet at:

http://publishing.grolier.com

Series editor: Rachel Cooke
Art director: Robert Walster
Designer: Mo Choy
Series consultant: Sally Nankivell-Aston

ISBN 0-516-21175-7 (lib. bdg.) 0-516-26338-2 (pbk.)
A CIP catalog record
for this book is available from
the Library of Congress.

Printed in Malaysia
Photographic acknowledgments:
Cover and title page: NHPA/B. Jones and M. Shimlock
Bruce Coleman Limited pp. 7c, 12l, 13tl, 19tl, 23tr (Kim Taylor), 8b (Rod Williams), 9l (Fred Breummer), 13c (Frans Lauting),
13br, 19b (Hans Reinhard), 16, 17t (Trevor Barrett), 18tl, 18tc, 18tr, 19tr (Jane Burton), 25l (Andrew Purcell), 27l (Steven C. Kaufman);
Frank Lane Picture Agency p. 24tr (B. Borrell);
NHPA pp. 6tr (Daryl Balfour), 6cr (Roger Tidman), 15l (John Shaws), 15r (David E. Myers), 24tl (A.N.T.), 25r (J. & M. Bain), 27r (Stephen Dalton);
Oxford Scientific Films pp. 5 & 10r (Stan Osolinski), 6 br (Okapia/W. Wisniewski), 7l (Animals Animals/Robert Maier), 7r (Raymond Blyth),
10l (Barrie Watts), 11tr (Stephen Dalton), 10cr (Kenneth Day), 18b (Michael Leach), 20t (Max Gibbs), 22 (London Scientific Films),
23l, 23cr (J.A.L. Cooke), 23cl (Peter Parks), 26l (Owen Newman), 26r (Konrad Nothe), 23r;
Still Pictures pp. 9r (Bruno Naso), 14l, 21tl (Norbert Wu), 14tr (Gilles Martin), 17b (R. Leguen);
Telegraph Colour Library pp. 11l (Planet Earth/Doug Perrine), 21tr (Planet Earth/Peter David), 24b (Planet Earth/Norbert Wu), 8t, 21b.
All other photographs by Ray Moller.

Contents

Backbones

Can you feel the knobby row of bones down the middle of your back? It is called your **backbone**.

You are a human being. Human beings belong to a group of animals with backbones.

a giraffe

a snake

a seagull

A giraffe, a snake, and a seagull all have backbones.

These animals do not have backbones:

a snail

a bee

a spider

All animals can be put into one of these two big groups — animals with backbones or animals without backbones.

There are many other ways of grouping animals together.
We will look at some of them in this book.

💡 **THINK ABOUT IT!**

Your backbone is part of your skeleton. What do you think you would look like without a **skeleton** of strong bones inside your body?

Mammals

Human beings belong to a group of animals called **mammals**. Mammals all have some hair or fur.

All baby mammals, such as this young chimpanzee, drink milk from their mothers. They need to be fed and looked after as soon as they are born. Only a very few baby mammals hatch from eggs.

LOOK AGAIN

Look again at page 6. Do mammals have backbones?

8

Monkeys and gibbons are mammals, too.

Troops of macaque monkeys live, play, and eat together.

💡 THINK ABOUT IT!

In what ways do you look like these apes and monkeys? How are you different?

A tiny baby gibbon clings to its mother's fur while she leaps through the trees. It can't look after itself until it is about eight years old.

9

Great and Small

All the animals on these pages are mammals. They look quite different from humans, but they all have hair or fur, and they all feed their babies with milk.

An elephant is the largest mammal that lives on land.

A pygmy shrew is the smallest.

 **LOOK AGAIN**

Look again at page 6 to find the tallest mammal.

A whale is the biggest mammal of all. It comes up from underwater to breathe air. A baby whale swims the moment it is born, but its mother still looks after it and feeds it with her milk.

A bat is a mammal that can fly.

Tiny baby kangaroos, called joeys, stay in their mother's pouch until they are old enough to jump away by themselves.

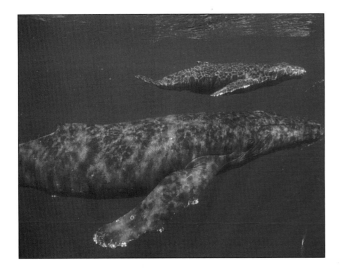

TRY IT OUT!

Cut out pictures of animals and put them into 2 groups — those that are mammals and those that are not mammals.

Birds

Birds are another group of animals with backbones. But one thing makes birds different from any other animal— birds are the only animals with feathers!

Long wing and tail feathers help a bird fly.

Small feathers cover the body.

Soft, fluffy feathers called *down* grow under the body feathers and help keep a bird warm.

TRY IT OUT!

Collect some feathers when you are outside. Are they body or flight feathers? Rub a feather down from its tip. What happens? Smooth it up toward the tip. What happens now?

Birds' wings are like strong arms. Small birds, like this robin, flap their wings very fast to fly.

An albatross flaps its long wings slowly and then spreads them out and floats through the air.

All birds lay eggs. When the baby birds hatch, they are covered in fluffy down. Their other feathers grow later.

13

All Kinds of Birds

Not all birds can fly. Penguins cannot fly, but they are excellent swimmers. It's a good thing their feathers are **waterproof**!

Some birds have amazingly colorful feathers to help them attract a **mate**. The colorful birds shown here are rainbow lories.

 **TRY IT OUT!**

Put some drops of water on one of the feathers you have collected. Shake the feather. What happens to the water?

Birds have differently shaped beaks
to help them eat their food.
A duck's beak is a good
shape for scooping
food out of water.
An eagle uses its
hooked beak for
hunting, and eating meat.

Birds have differently shaped feet, too.
Ducks have webbed feet for swimming.
How do you think an eagle
uses its fiercely sharp talons?

💡 THINK ABOUT IT!

How can we tell one kind of bird from another just by looking at them?

Reptiles

Lizards, alligators, snakes, and turtles all belong to a group of animals with backbones called **reptiles**. They have dry, scaly, waterproof skin.

Reptiles use **energy** from the sun to keep warm.
They still need energy from food to move and breathe, but they don't have to eat nearly as much as mammals and birds do.

This lizard is basking in the sun to get warm.
If the sun gets too hot, the lizard will hide in the shade.

Alligators have nostrils on top of their noses. When they swim in rivers, their nostrils stick up out of the water so they can still breathe the air.

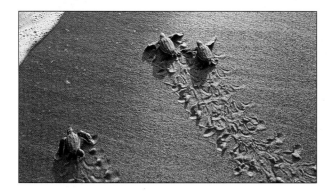

Reptiles lay eggs.
Turtles lay their eggs in the sand.
When the baby turtles hatch, they have to make a long and dangerous journey down to the sea.

👁 LOOK AGAIN

Look again at page 6. What reptile can you see with no legs?
Look again at page 13 to find another group of animals that lay eggs.

Amphibians

Amphibians are a special group of animals with backbones.
They live underwater for the first part of their lives.
When they are fully grown, they can live in water and on land.

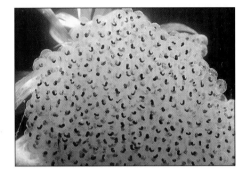

Frogs lay their eggs, called **spawn**, underwater.

The eggs hatch into tadpoles, which live and breathe underwater like tiny fish.

Soon the tadpoles lose their tails, grow four legs, and begin to look like little frogs.

Frogs breathe out of water. They swim in ponds or leap on land.

Toads, newts, and salamanders are all amphibians.

Toads shoot out their long, sticky tongues to catch their food.

You can tell a newt by its flat tail. Newts hide in cracks between rocks and sleep all winter.

Salamanders have small weak legs. They slither along the ground like a snake.

LOOK AGAIN

Look at page 16 to find an animal that looks quite similar to newts and salamanders. How can you tell the difference between them?

Fish

Fish are another group of animals with backbones. They spend their whole lives underwater.

Fish have **gills** on each side of their head. These let them breathe underwater.

fin ——————————————

gill ——————————

THINK ABOUT IT!

Why can't you stay underwater for very long when you go swimming?

Most fish, like this salmon, have streamlined bodies, strong tails, and fins.

An angler fish stays still to catch fish with the glowing "rod and line" on its head.

Which of these two fish has the best shape for swimming fast through water?

💡 THINK ABOUT IT!

Fish have slippery overlapping scales. Why do you think some roof tiles overlap each other in a fish-scale pattern like this?

Insects

Insects are a group of animals that live in every corner of the earth, even on other animals and people!

_____ antenna

wing

👁 LOOK AGAIN

Look again at page 7 to find out if insects, like this bee, have a backbone.

You have bones inside your body. Insects have a hard case on the outside of their bodies to protect them.

All insects have three parts to their bodies and six legs. Can you count the body parts and legs on this bee?

Many insects have wings and can fly.

💡 THINK ABOUT IT!

A spider has eight legs. Do you think a spider is an insect?

antenna

Insects use their **antennae** to smell, taste, and feel what is happening all around them.

Nearly all insects lay eggs. Most hatch from the eggs as **larvae**, then completely change to become adults.

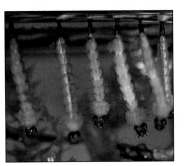

A gnat lays its eggs in the water.

Larvae hatch from the eggs.

A larva becomes a **pupa**.

The pupa splits open and a gnat flies away.

 TRY IT OUT!

Look for insects on and under leaves, under stones, or in the ground. Now study one of them more closely: Put some dirt in the bottom of a glass jar. Add a few leaves from where you have spotted your insect. Gently brush the insect into the jar. Cover the jar with a lid that has holes to let air in. After you have looked at the insect, put it back where you found it.

23

Soft Bodies and Shells

All the creatures on these two pages have soft bodies and no backbones.

A slug makes a slimy trail to slither along.

Earthworms wriggle through dirt, eating it as they go.

An octopus can squash its soft body into very small spaces.

24

All the animals on this page have shells to protect their soft bodies.

This is the mouth of an enormous shell. Inside it is the soft body of a giant clam. It can close its shell when there is danger nearby.

A crab wears a tough coat on its back and legs like a suit of armor.

👁 LOOK AGAIN

Look again at page 22 to find a group of animals that have a hard case on the outside of their bodies to protect them, too. Look again at page 7 to find another animal with a shell to protect its soft body.

Looking After Animals

People can put animals in danger, but they can help them, too. Animals need a safe place to live and to find food.

Woodland creatures, such as this dormouse, are in danger when woods are cut down. **Nature reserves** give them a safe place to live.

Rain forest creatures, such as the gorilla, have nowhere to live if the forests are cut down. People must protect the rain forests in order to protect the animals.

💡 THINK ABOUT IT!

Hunters killed all the wild Arabian oryx in the desert where they lived. Only a few were left living in zoos. Now oryx born in zoos have been taken back to the wild. Today, there is a small herd of wild oryx living in the desert again.

🖐 TRY IT OUT!

Make a bird feeder out of reach of hungry cats. In the winter, put some wild bird food and some water in it. Watch all the different birds that visit.
If you have a garden, leave a wild place for insects to live. These insects are food for other animals, too.

Useful Words

Amphibians Amphibians are a group of animals with backbones. They live underwater for the first part of their lives. When fully grown, they breathe out of water and can live on land.

Antennae Antennae are long, thin feelers on the heads of insects and some other animals without backbones. They use them to smell, taste, and feel the world around them.

Backbone Every animal with a skeleton inside its body has a flexible row of bones down the center of its back called a backbone.

Birds Birds are a group of animals with backbones. They have feathers and wings, and they lay eggs.

Energy Animals use energy from the food they eat and from the sun to keep warm, grow, and move.

Fish Fish are a group of animals with backbones. They can only live underwater. They breathe through gills.

Gills Fish breathe through two gills, one of each side of their head.

Insects Insects are an animal group with no backbone. Their bodies are divided into three parts and protected by a hard case. They have six legs.

Larvae Most insects hatch from eggs as larvae (one newly hatched insect is called a larva). Larvae usually look quite different from the adults they grow into. For example, a caterpillar is the larva of a butterfly.

Mammals Mammals are a group of animals with backbones. They have some hair or fur. Baby mammals drink milk from their mothers.

Mate When animals become adults, they look for a mate so that they can produce babies. A male animal has a female mate.

Nature reserves Nature reserves are special places where plants and animals are protected to help them grow and live in safety.

Pupa Some insects become a pupa while they are making the huge change from a larva to an adult. A caterpillar becomes a pupa while it is changing into a butterfly.

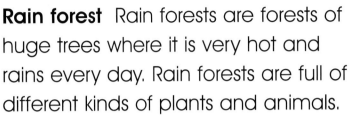

Rain forest Rain forests are forests of huge trees where it is very hot and rains every day. Rain forests are full of different kinds of plants and animals.

Reptiles Reptiles are a group of animals with backbones, with scaly, waterproof skin. They breathe air, and some live on land and others in water.

Skeleton Animals with backbones have a skeleton of strong bones under their skin to support their bodies.

Spawn Eggs laid in a mass in water are called spawn. Frogs' eggs are called frogspawn.

Waterproof Waterproof coverings keep water out. A waterproof raincoat keeps you dry in the rain. Waterproof feathers help keep birds dry.

Index

About This Book

Children are natural scientists. They learn by touching, noticing, asking questions, and trying things out for themselves. The books in the *It's Science!* series are designed for the way children learn. Familiar objects are used as starting points for further learning. *All Kinds of Animals* starts with a child and explores the ways we group animals.

Each double-page spread introduces a new topic, such as mammals or insects. Information is given, questions asked, and activities suggested that encourage children to make discoveries and develop new ideas for themselves.
Look out for these panels throughout the book:

TRY IT OUT! indicates a simple activity, using safe materials, that proves or explores a point.
THINK ABOUT IT! indicates a question inspired by the information on the page but that points the reader to areas not covered in the book.
LOOK AGAIN introduces a cross-referencing activity that links themes and facts through the book.

Encourage children not to take the familiar world for granted. Point things out, ask questions, and enjoy making scientific discoveries together.